ROSALIE'S GUIDE TO
RESTAURANTS
in the North End
of Boston

BY

ROSALIE TAGG MASELLA

CONTENTS

PARKING

- Due to the "Big Dig", parking is limited on Atlantic Avenue under the expressway.

- "Visitor" designated parking spaces are available on selected streets.

- On-street parking spaces ("visitor" or meter) typically have a 2-hour limit during the day.

- Meter parking requires 8 quarters for a 2-hour limit.

- Check with your restaurant for validated parking.

PARKING LOTS

COMMERCIAL STREET
Kinney Garage .... between Prince St. and Hull St.

Fitz Inn .... between Hull St. and Charter St.

Laz Parking .... between Clark St. and Fleet St.

Fitz Inn .... between Eastern St. and Clark St.

COOPER STREET
Pinstripe .... between Endicott St. and Margin St.

FANEUIL HALL AREA
Dock Square .... Clinton St. and Surface Road

Gov't Center .... New Sudbury St., Congress St.,
New Chardon St.

Parcel 7 .... New Sudbury St., Congress St.,
Hanover St.

Center Plaza .... Somerset St. and Tremont St.

All Right .... Under X-Way

Kinney Haymarket ...... N. Washington St. and
New Chardon St.

75 State St. .... Corner of Broad St. and State St.

ATLANTIC AVENUE
Rowes Wharf .... 50 Rowes Wharf on Atlantic Ave.

Boston Harbor Garage . Near Aquarium - Milk St. and
Atlantic Ave.

RESTAURANTS
LISTED BY STREET

CAUSEWAY STREET
>FILIPPO'S BISTRO
>FILIPPO RESTAURANT

ENDICOTT STREET
>MANGIA-MANGIA
>MASIMINO'S CUCINA ITALIANA
>PAT'S PUSHCART

FLEET STREET
>LA SUMMA

HANOVER STREET
>ALLORO
>CAFFE DELLO SPORT
>CAFFE GRAFFITI
>CAFFE PARADISO
>CAFFE POMPEI
>CAFFE VITTORIA, INC.
>CANTINA ITALIANA
>CIBO
>CIRCLE PIZZA
>CONTRADA'S COFFEE SHOPPE
>DOLCE VITA CAFFE
>DOLCE VITA RESTAURANT
>D'PARMA
>FLORENTINE CAFE, INC.
>GALLERIA UMBERTO
>GIACOMO'S

HANOVER STREET
>IL BACIO
>IL FORNAIO
>IL PANINO EXPRESS
>IL VILLAGGIO

(cont'd)

6

LA FAMIGLIA SPAGNUOLO
LODO
LUCIA
MAURIZIO'S
MOTHER ANNA'S
PICCOLA VENEZIA
PIZZA RELLA
POMODORO
RISTORANTE BELLA VISTA
RISTORANTE ROSINA
RISTORANTE SARACENO
STANZA dei SIGARI
THE DAILY CATCH
TRATTORIA A SCALINATELLA
VADOPAZZO

JOE TECCE WAY
JOE TECCE'S

MECHANIC STREET
IDA'S

NORTH SQUARE
FIVE NORTH SQUARE

NORTH STREET
FLORENCE
MAMMA MARIA
NORTH STREET GRILLE
PICCOLO NIDO
RICARDO'S

NORTH WASHINGTON STREET
FRANCESCO'S
GROTTO LA STRADA
SABATINO'S

PARMENTER STREET
FRATELLI PAGLIUCA
TRATTORIA IL PANINO

cont'd

Restaurants by Street (cont'd)

PRINCE STREET
 ARTU
 ASSAGGIO
 G'VANNI'S
 MONICA'S KITCHEN
 SAGE

RICHMOND STREET
 ARMIDA'S
 MONICA'S
 VILLA-FRANCESCA

SALEM STREET
 ANTICO FORNO
 AL DENTE
 D'AMORE'S
 DINO'S
 ERNESTO'S
 LA FAMIGLIA GIORGIO'S
 LO CONTE'S
 L'OSTERIA
 MARCUCCIO'S
 NICOLE
 PUSHCART CAFFE
 RABIA'S
 RISTORANTE EUNO
 TERRAMIA
 THEO'S COZY CORNER
 TRATTORIA LORENZO
 TUTTO MARE

THATCHER STREET
 PIZZERIA REGINA

BAKERIES
IN THE
NORTH END

A. BOSCHETTO'S

158 Salem Street
(617) 523-9350
7AM-4PM (Mon.-Sat.)
6AM-Noon (Sun.)

A. BOVA AND SONS

134 Salem Street
(617) 523-5601
Open 24hrs. - 7 days

BISCOTTI'S

95 Salem Street
(617) 227-8365
8AM-9PM (Sun.-Fri.)
8AM-Midnight (Sat.)

J. PACE AND SON

41 Cross Street
(617) 227-9673
7AM-7PM (Mon.-Sat.)
8AM-5PM (Sun.)

cont'd

MARIA'S PASTRY SHOP
46 Cross Street
(617) 523-1196
6AM-6PM

MIKE'S PASTRY, INC.
300 Hanover Street
(617) 742-3050
8AM-9PM (Mon, Wed., Thurs.)
10AM-6PM (Tues.)
9AM-10PM (Fri.)
8AM-11PM (Sat.)
8AM-10PM (Sun.)

MODERN PASTRY SHOP, INC.
257 Hanover Street
(617) 523-3783
8AM-10PM

PARZIALE'S BAKERY
80 Prince Street
(617) 523-6368
7:30AM-6PM (Mon.-Sat.)
7:30AM-2PM (Sun.)

DELICATESSEN'S IN THE NORTH END

SALUMERIA ITALIANA
151 Richmond Street
(800) 400-5916
8AM-6PM (Daily)
8AM-7PM (Fri.)
Closed Sunday

MAURIZIO'S
20 Fleet Street
(617) 726-1133
Noon-6PM (Sun.-Mon.)
10AM-7PM (Tues.-Sat.)

MONICA'S SALUMERIA
130 Salem Street
(617) 742-4101
11AM-8PM (Daily)
9:30AM-8PM (Sat.)

J. PACE
41 Cross Street
(617) 227-9673
7AM-7PM (Mon.-Sat.)
8AM-5PM (Sun.)

cont'd

Deli's (cont'd)

POLCARI'S
105 Salem Street
(617) 227-0786
8:30AM-6PM (Daily)
Closed Sunday

SALUMERIA TOSCANNA
272 Hanover Street
(617) 720-4243
10AM-10PM (Daily)

RESTAURANTS
in the
NORTH END
of
BOSTON

AL DENTE RESTAURANT

109 Salem Street
(617) 523-0990

Reservations: Recommended
Casual attire
Entree prices start at: $6.95
AMEX, VISA/MC

"Once you try us, you'll be back again" is the motto of **AL DENTE**. A charming restaurant which seats 50 people, the cuisine features chicken, veal, shrimp and of course, pasta. Authentic Italian food is prepared with the freshest ingredients. Daily specials.

Lunch: 11AM-4PM
Dinner: 4PM-10PM (Mon.-Thurs.)
4PM-11PM (Fri.,Sat.,Sun.)

ALLORO

351 Hanover Street
(617) 523-9268

Reservations: Recommended
Casual attire
Entree prices start at: $7.95
AMEX, VISA/MC

Small and efficient, **ALLORO** offers a variety of dishes, including the Gamberetti grilled shrimp served with a salad of fennel and olives atop a chick pea fritter. A house specialty is a seafood entree consisting of shrimp, clams, mussels and calamari served over a bed of linguini in a tomato broth.

Hours: 5PM-10:30PM (Tues.-Thurs.)
5PM-11PM (Fri.-Sat.)
Noon-10PM (Sun.)
Closed Monday

ANTICO FORNO

93 Salem Street
(617) 723-6733

Reservations: Recommended
Casual attire
Entree prices start at: $7.00
VISA/MC

If you are looking for a great meal in a casual, relaxed atmosphere, **ANTICO FORNO** is the place! The portions are generous and the prices are reasonable. A wonderful antique wood-burning oven warms your heart the minute you see it. It is said to have the best gourmet pizza in the North End.

Lunch: 11:30AM-3:30PM
Dinner: 3:30PM-10PM (Mon.-Thurs.)
3:30PM-10:30PM (Fri.-Sat.)
noon-10PM (Sun.)

ARMIDA'S

135 Richmond Street
(617) 523-9545

Reservations: Recommended
Casual attire
Entree prices start at: $13.95
AMEX, VISA/MC

For those looking for a charming and delightful atmosphere and delicious cuisine, make a reservation at **ARMIDA'S.** The 50-seat restaurant's specialty of the house is chicken or veal Roberto (chicken or veal sauteed in white wine, served with artichoke hearts and mushrooms) Available for private parties and events on Wednesdays, Thursdays, and Fridays.

5PM-10PM (Wed., Thurs., Fri., Sat.)

ARTÚ

6 Prince Street
(617) 742-4336

Reservations: Recommended
Casual attire
Entree prices start at: $8.75
MC/VISA

ARTÚ serves traditional Italian specialties in
an extremely pleasant environment. It touts
that it serves the best meat sandwich in
Boston! One of the flavorful dishes is Pollo
Farcito alla Donato (chicken breast stuffed
with prosciutto, spinach and cheese, breaded
and fried.) The locals gravitate to this
popular rosticceria and trattoria.

Open Daily
Lunch: 11AM-4PM
Dinner: 4PM-11PM

ASSAGGIO RESTAURANT

29 Prince Street
(617) 227-7380

Reservations: Recommended
Casual attire
Entree prices start at: $8.95
AMEX, VISA/MC

ASSAGGIO is a newly established Italian restaurant with a French twist. Near the corner of Prince Street and Hanover Street, it provides a warm and romantic atmosphere with exquisite food coupled with a selection of over 60 wines served by the glass or 150 wines by the bottle.There is a full bar. Available for private parties and events.

Open Daily
Lunch: Noon-4PM
Dinner: 4PM-Midnight

CAFFÉ DELLO SPORT

308 Hanover Street
(617) 523-5063

Casual attire
Credit cards not accepted

CAFFÉ DELLO SPORT is a neat, casual
Italian restaurant where you can order small
individual pizzas, focaccia, hot Italian sandwiches,
cakes or tiramisu. They offer beer, wine and
cordials. A fun place to meet and have a light bite.

Open Daily
6:30AM-1AM

CAFFÉ GRAFFITI

307 Hanover Street
(617) 367-3016

Casual attire
Credit cards not accepted

CAFFÉ GRAFFITI is a comfortable stop
anytime for a cappuccino or espresso.
It's a pleasant cafe for an after dinner dessert
and a delicious finale to your evening.
Enjoy the cafe mocha (hot or iced), cake,
pastry, soda, beer, wine and cordials.

Open Daily
6AM-Midnight

CAFFÉ PARADISO

253-255 Hanover Street
(617) 742-1768

Casual attire
Prices start at: $5.00
All major credit cards accepted

Located on Boston's historic Freedom Trail since 1962, **CAFFÉ PARADISO** is an authentic Italian cafe. It's a great place to enjoy cappuccino, espresso, a good variety of beer, wine, pastry and cake. A gas fireplace downstairs adds a nice warm touch to this busy cafe. Available for private parties and events.

Open Daily
7AM-2AM

CAFFÉ POMPEI

280 Hanover Street
(617) 227-1562

Casual attire
Entree prices start at: $6.00
VISA/MC

Experience an Italian coffee bar with a
nightclub ambiance at **CAFFÉ POMPEI.**
After the clubs close, this is the place to go
until 4 am! There is a full menu at all times
which includes unbelievable pizza. Try their
famous banana ice cream. Top this off with
iced or hot cappuccino. Beer and wine served
until midnight. A super spot to meet!

Open Daily
8:30AM-4AM

CAFFÉ VITTORIA, INC.

296 Hanover Street
(617) 227-7606

Casual attire
Prices start at: $3.00
Credit cards not accepted

CAFFÉ VITTORIA is Boston's oldest cafe.
It features four levels to enjoy cappuccino,
freshly baked pastries and a full assortment of
liqueurs. This is a must stop for dessert dining!

Open Daily
8AM-Midnight

CANTINA ITALIANA

346 Hanover Street
(617) 723-4577

Reservations: Recommended
Valet parking available after 5PM
Casual attire
Entree prices start at: $12.00
All major credit cards accepted

CANTINA ITALIANA is one of the oldest restaurants in the North End, established in 1931. There are cozy booths within this very warm and comfortable restaurant. It's a nice place to take a date. The pasta is home-made and all food is cooked to order. A specialty is the polla alla franco (boneless breast of chicken, scallops, mushrooms and leeks in a vermouth and light cream sauce with fettucine). They offer catering to homes and offices for all occasions. Available for private parties and events.

Hours: 4PM-11PM (Mon.-Sat.)
Noon-10:00PM (Sun.)

CIBO

326 Hanover Street
(617) 557-9248

Reservations: Recommended
Casual attire
Entree prices start at: $9.95
VISA/MC

CIBO serves fresh, imaginative vegetarian dishes as well as a nice variety of chicken, veal and seafood. The chef creates authentic Italian cuisine and presents it attractively. Daily Italian Nouveau specials. Perky, delightful atmosphere. Available for private parties and events.

5PM-10PM (Mon.-Thurs.)
5PM-11PM (Fri.)
Noon-11PM (Sat.)
Noon-10PM (Sun.)

CIRCLE PIZZA

361 Hanover Street
(617) 523-8787

Casual attire
Entree prices start at: $3.75
Credit cards not accepted

CIRCLE PIZZA has been making and serving pizza, sandwiches and calzones for over 30 years. For a special treat, try the chicken, broccoli and cheese calzone. Beer, wine, soda, coffee and tea are available. Dine-in, take-out, or call for delivery.

Open Daily
Noon-10PM

CONTRADA'S COFFEE SHOPPE

396 Hanover Street
(617) 367-2251

Casual attire
Credit cards not accepted

CONTRADA'S is a coffee lover's dream.
There is a wide selection of gourmet coffee
and tea. Also available are donuts, muffins,
"finagle a bagel," cakes and breakfast
sandwiches, plus much more.

Hours: 6AM-3PM (Mon.-Sat.)
6AM-1PM (Sun.)

D'AMORE'S RESTAURANT

76 Salem Street
(617) 523-8820

Reservations: Recommended
Casual attire
Entree prices start at: $7.50
All major credit cards accepted

D'AMORE'S, established in 1974, is one of the oldest restaurants in the North End and is owner operated. The atmosphere is cozy. In the spring and summer the windows slide open to provide a fresh air setting. Serving Northern and Southern Italian cuisine, all food is cooked to order. Take advantage of the early dinner specials available Monday - Friday from 3PM-7PM and Sunday until 5PM.

Lunch: 11:30AM-3PM
Dinner: 3PM-10PM (Mon.-Sat.)
11:30AM-9:30PM (Sun.)

DINO'S CAFE

141 Salem Street
(617) 227-1991

Casual attire
Credit cards not accepted

DINO'S CAFE is on the corner of Salem Street
and Prince Street. It's a great place for pizza,
pasta and gigantic 16-inch subs on freshly
baked french bread. The chefs are upbeat
and will work very efficiently to get
your order to you quickly.

Open daily
12noon-10pm

DOLCE VITA CAFFE

237 Hanover Street
(617) 720-0422

Casual attire
All major credit cards accepted

Specializing in home-made desserts that will
bring you a taste of Italy, **DOLCE VITA** is a
great meeting place. Indulge in tiramisu, creme
caramel, chocolate mousse, chocolate raspberry
torte, cappuccino torte or a delicious canoli.
Beer, wine, and liqueurs are available.

Open Daily
9AM-Midnight

DOLCE VITA RESTAURANT

237 Hanover Street
(617) 720-0422

Reservations: Recommended
Casual attire
Entree prices start at: $10.00
All major credit cards accepted

Dine in warmth and elegance in this upstairs
dining room overlooking Hanover Street.
Specialties of the house include home-made
pasta, seafood, veal and chicken all tastefully
presented. **DOLCE VITA** creates traditional
dishes with a European flair.

Open Daily
Lunch: 11AM-3PM
Dinner: 3PM-11PM

DOM'S

100 Salem St.
(617) 367-8979

Reservations: Recommended
Casual attire
Entree prices start at: $19.00
All major credit cards accepted

Set back a little from Salem Street is this celebrated restaurant. At **DOM'S**, you may order either Northern or Southern Italian dishes. There is a plethora of seafood including several of Boston's best lobster choices. Steak and rack of lamb are always moist and tender. Dom regularly patrols his tables to make certain that everyone is pleased with their meal. Relaxed dining in a cordial environment. Available for private parties and events.

Open Daily
5PM-11PM

D'PARMA RISTORANTE

456 Hanover Street
(617) 523-4205

Reservations: Recommended
Casual attire
Entree prices start at: $6.95
VISA/MC

Generous portions at reasonable prices await you at **D'PARMA.** Try the linguine, gnocchi, or the exceptional calamari ravioli. Eat in or take out. Free parking after 6PM at the gas station across the street.

Open Daily
Lunch: 10AM-3PM
Dinner: 4PM-11PM

ERNESTO'S PIZZA

69 Salem Street
(617) 523-1373

Casual attire
Entree prices start at:
$8.50 (whole Pizza)
$1.85 (slice)
Credit cards not accepted

ERNESTO'S serves old world pizza and calzones. There are 20 varieties of pizza, good Italian sandwiches, and 10 different kinds of calzones. A popular parlor for quick and delicious food, beer, and wine.

Open Daily
10AM-11PM

FILIPPO'S BOSTON GARDEN BISTRO

287 Causeway Street
(617) 742-4142

Reservations: Recommended
Casual attire
Entree prices start at: $4.50
Credit cards not accepted

If you are keen on reminiscing about the old Boston Garden, **FILIPPO'S BOSTON GARDEN BISTRO** is the place! Have a "Celtic Pride" pizza, the "Big Puck" calzone, a "Scully Square" sandwich, "North Station" pasta or the "Bird's Nest" salad. The bar and dining room are decorated with authentic memorabilia from the Old Garden. The prices are in line with those back in the days of Bird and Orr.

Hours: 11:30AM-12:30AM (Sun.-Thurs.)
11:30AM-1:30AM (Fri.-Sat.)

FILIPPO RISTORANTE

283 Causeway Street
(617) 742-4143

Reservations: Recommended
Valet parking available
Dressy casual
Entree prices start at: $8.75
AMEX, VISA/MC

On the Freedom Trail and close to the Fleet Center, **FILIPPO'S** location is convenient for all. The traditional menu offers innovative dishes which are complemented by a distinctive selection of wines and spirits. Warm and casually elegant describes the ambiance. Available for private parties and events.

Hours: 11:30AM-10:30PM (Tues. - Sun.)
Closed Monday

FIVE NORTH SQUARE ITALIAN RESTAURANT

5 North Square
(617) 720-1050

Reservations: Recommended
Casual attire
Entree prices start at: $12.95
All major credit cards accepted

FIVE NORTH SQUARE, located on the Freedom Trail next to the Paul Revere house, overlooks the oldest public square in the country. The menu is impressive, offering a diversity of traditional Italian fare in a lovely Mediterranean setting. There is seating for 30 people on the first floor, 75 people on the second floor. Available for private parties and events.

Open Daily
Lunch: 11:30AM-3PM
Dinner: 5PM-11PM

FLORENTINE CAFE, INC.

333 Hanover Street
(617) 227-1777

Reservations: Not accepted
Casual attire
Entree prices start at: $13.00
All major credit cards accepted

The **FLORENTINE CAFE** opened shortly after prohibition. It features a wonderfully large hand-crafted walnut bar. Full bar service is available. They offer a delightful bistro menu with gourmet Italian cuisine. In addition, baked stuffed lobster is a house specialty. Available for private parties and events.

Open Daily
Noon-1AM

FLORENCE RESTAURANT

190 North Street
(617) 523-4480

Reservations: Recommended
Casual attire
Entree prices start at: $12.95
All major credit cards accepted

FLORENCE RESTAURANT is located near the Paul Revere house. Specialties of this relaxed and comfortable restaurant include veal, veal chops, swordfish, mussels and all varieties of tasty and well presented pasta dishes. The staff is amicable and efficient. Available for private parties and events.

Open Daily
Lunch: 11AM-3PM
Dinner: 3PM-11PM

FRANCESCO'S

90 North Washington Street
(617) 557-0920

Reservations: Recommended
Casual attire
Entree prices start at: $8.95
All major credit cards accepted

FRANCESCO'S is a comfortable family
restaurant located close to the Fleet Center,
the late-night hours of operation are convenient
for hungry event-goers! The menu includes
a large variety of pizza, as well as in-house roasted
turkey and roast beef. Full liquor license.
Available for private parties and events.

Hours: 11:30AM-12 Midnight (Mon.-Thurs.)
11:30AM-2AM (Fri.-Sat.)
Closed Sunday

FRATELLI PAGLIUCA

14 Parmenter Street
(617) 367-1504

Reservations: Recommended
Casual attire
Entree prices start at: $8.00
AMEX, VISA/MC, DINERS

FRATELLI PAGLIUCA has been owned and operated by the Pagliuca family since 1986, when they brought their homeland recipes from Montefalcione Avellino, Italy. They created a homey and personal restaurant full of old world charm. Specialties are pasta and meat entrees such as chicken campagna ("on the farm"), roast veal and much more.

Lunch: 11AM-4PM
Dinner: 4PM-10PM (Sun.-Thurs.)
4PM-11PM (Fri.-Sat.)

GALLERIA UMBERTO

289 Hanover Street
(617) 227-5709

Casual attire
Credit cards not accepted

Come to this fun restaurant and bring the family! **GALLERIA UMBERTO** serves specialties such as pan pizza, calzones and arancini. The pan pizza is very popular with folks who want to have a pizza party at home. Call ahead to order. Beer and wine available.

Open Daily
11AM-2:30PM
Closed July

GIACOMO'S RISTORANTE

355 Hanover Street
(617) 523-9026

Reservations not accepted
Casual attire
Entree prices start at: $9.95
Credit cards not accepted

This casual restaurant offers authentic Southern Italian cuisine. Seafood specialties include clams, mussels, shrimp, scallops and calamari served over linguini, grilled swordfish, salmon and tuna. **GIACOMO'S** pasta selections give you a choice of five different sauces. It is famous for the scrumptious pumpkin tortellini in a fresh sage mascarpone cheese sauce.

Hours: 5PM-10PM (Mon.-Thurs.)
5PM-10:30PM (Fri.-Sat.)
4PM-10PM (Sun.)

GROTTO LA STRADA

111 North Washington Street
(617) 742-2998 or (617) 523-9777

Reservations: Recommended
Casual attire
Entree prices start at: $8.95
VISA/MC

GROTTO LA STRADA has been a North
End landmark for over 25 years. Enjoy the
enormous and delicious pork chops served
with fried potatoes which has been an
exceptional house specialty for years.
The menu offers interesting Northern and
Southern Italian cuisine. Specials offered
every day in this comfortable and
charming restaurant.

Hours: 4PM-10PM (Mon.-Thurs.)
4PM-11PM (Fri.-Sat.)
Noon-10PM (Sun.)

G'VANNI'S
2 Prince Street
(617) 523-0107

Reservations: Recommended
Casual attire
Entree prices start at: $10.95
All major credit cards accepted

Enjoy fine traditional Northern Italian
cuisine at this charming, intimate restaurant. Although seafood Italiana is a specialty of the house at **G'Vanni's**, the
creative and innovative menu offers many
delicious choices. The food is classic and
consistent. Daily specials.
Established 1982.

Open Daily
Lunch: 11AM-3PM
Dinner: 4PM-11PM

IDA'S RESTAURANT

1 Mechanic Street
(617) 523-0015

Reservations: Recommended
Entree prices start at: $9.95
Credit cards not accepted

Casual and friendly describes this down-to-earth cozy Italian restaurant. Located only a few steps off Hanover Street, **IDA'S** serves plenty of fine food cooked fresh everyday. Roast veal is a specialty but many other delicious dishes await you. All entrees served with pasta and salad. Established 1951. Available for private parties and events.

Open Mon.-Sat.
Hours: 5PM-10:00PM
Closed Sunday
Closed July

IL BACIO

226 Hanover Street
(617) 742-9200

Reservations: Recommended
Casual attire
Entree prices start at: $9.00
All major credit cards accepted

IL BACIO is an elegant restaurant with a marble-topped mahogany bar and mahogany cafe tables with comfortable rattan chairs. Offering a full service bar with 100 wines from Italy and California, it is modeled after Harry's American Bar in Florence, Italy. The food is both Northern and Southern Italian, with an emphasis on seafood. It is an open air restaurant which accommodates 80 people on the first floor and 60 on the lower level. Available for private parties and events.

Open Daily
Lunch: Noon-4PM
Dinner: 4PM-10PM (Sun.-Thurs.)
4PM-11PM (Fri.-Sat.)

IL FORNAIO

221 Hanover Street
(617) 742-3394

Casual attire
All major credit cards accepted

IL FORNAIO reminds one of the simple rhythm of older times. It is a friendly grocery store which has tables and chairs. There are wonderful subs as well as pizza. Try a pasta or garden pizza! In the deli section you'll find Italian cheeses, meats, oils, porchetta, arancini and fantastic Italian bread. Delivery available. A class is offered once a month on bread and pizza making. Call for information.

Open Daily
Hours: 8AM-8PM

IL PANINO EXPRESS

264-266 Hanover Street
(617) 720-5720

Casual attire
Entree prices start at: $4.25
Credit cards not accepted

The North End's only cafeteria-style fast food
Italian restaurant, **IL PANINO** cooks all food
fresh daily. It's a great family place, airy, fast
and pleasant. Choose from among pizza,
calzone, salad, soup, penne, fusilli, or lasagna.
Beer and wine. Fun atmosphere with Italian
music in the background. Part of the Trattoria
Il Panino restaurant group.

Open Daily
11AM-11PM

IL VILLAGGIO

230 Hanover Street
(617) 367-2824

Reservations: Recommended
Casual attire
Entree prices start at: $8.95
AMEX, VISA/MC

IL VILLAGGIO (the village) presents its food
with a Northern Italian influence. Although the
specialty is seafood, other delicious menu
selections include chicken, veal, pasta and the
gnocchi is numero uno! Take a fantasy trip to
Italy and order their risotto frutti d'mare.

Hours: 10AM-10PM (Mon.-Thurs.)
10AM-11PM (Fri.,Sat.,Sun.)

JOE TECCE'S

61 Joe Tecce Way
(formerly N. Washington St.)
(617) 742-6210

Reservations: Recommended
Casual attire
Entree prices start at: $9.95
AMEX, VISA/MC

Family owned and operated since 1948,
JOE TECCE'S is a landmark in the North End.
Northern and Southern Italian cuisine are
served in a casual, truly relaxing atmosphere
with a European flavor. There are six tastefully
decorated dining rooms and two cocktail
bars. Children's menu. Smoking in cafe.
Available for private parties and events for
up to 325 people.

Open Daily
Lunch: 11:30AM-3PM
Dinner: 3PM-11PM

LA FAMIGLIA GIORGIO'S

112 Salem Street
(617) 367-6711

Reservations not accepted
Casual attire
Entree prices start at: $6.95
All major credit cards accepted

LA FAMIGLIA GIORGIO'S is an informal, family-style restaurant catering to families, students and tourists. There is an extensive menu of basic, simple, good Italian food and the portions are HUGE! Choose from a nice selection of wines to complement your meal.

Open Daily
Lunch: 11AM-3PM
Dinner: 3PM-Midnight

LA FAMIGLIA SPAGNUOLO

240 Hanover Street
(617) 742-0124

Reservations: Recommended
Casual attire
Entree prices start at: $7.95
All major credit cards accepted

LA FAMIGLIA SPAGNUOLO is an
original North End neighborhood restaurant.
The traditionally prepared Italian food is
reasonably priced and the portions are
substantial. After lunch or dinner, enjoy the
spumoni or sorbet with your coffee.
Full liquor license.

Open daily
11AM-11PM

LA SUMMA RESTAURANT

30 Fleet Street
(617) 523-9503

Reservations: Recommended
Casual attire
Entree prices start at: $10.95
All major credit cards accepted

Relax in one of the several intimate booths at this family owned and operated establishment. Enjoy your evening in a comfortable, unhurried atmosphere. All pasta is fresh every day and each meal is cooked to order. **LA SUMMA** uses no preservatives. If you have never dined in an Italian home, **LA SUMMA** is the place!

Open Daily
4PM-10PM
1:30PM-10PM (Sun.)

LO CONTE'S RESTAURANT

116 Salem Street
(617) 720-3550

Reservations: Recommended
Casual attire
Entree prices start at: $10.50
All major credit cards accepted

Charming, bright and cheery, with a friendly staff describes **LO CONTE'S.** Specialties of the house include cold antipasto, shrimp ravioli, filet of sole, gnocchi spezzatino, and a delicious combo of chicken, broccoli and ziti. It's a delightful place for a meal on a hurried day or evening.

Open Daily
11AM-10PM
11AM-11PM (Fri.-Sat.)

LODO

210 Hanover Street
(617) 720-0052

Casual attire
Entree prices start at: $10.00
All major credit cards accepted

At **LODO**, (<u>Lo</u>wer <u>Do</u>wntown) you experience the old world charm of the North End. Its granite structure has tall, 12 ft. ceilings and 9 ft. windows that provide fabulous views of Boston's financial district. The contemporary decor is unmistakably European. **LODO's** extensive menu offers old and new Mediterranean recipes all served with the freshest ingredients with attention to color and detail. The bread and desserts are all homemade. Cigars available. Upstairs smoking room. Available for private parties and events.

Open daily
11AM-12Midnight

L'OSTERIA
RESTAURANT

104 Salem Street
(617) 723-7847

Reservations: Recommended
Casual attire
Entree prices start at: $7.50
AMEX, VISA/MC, DINERS

L'OSTERIA offers quality cuisine at affordable prices. The friendly ambiance of the restaurant makes it an ideal spot for a business lunch, family dinner or an intimate dinner for two. The full, appetizing menu includes veal as well as chicken merenga and bocconcini di vitello triestini. Available for private parties and events.

Lunch: 11:45AM-3PM
Dinner: 3PM-10PM (Mon.-Fri.)
3PM-11PM (Sat.-Sun.)

LUCIA RISTORANTE

415 Hanover Street
(617) 367-2353

Reservations: Recommended
Valet parking available
Casual attire
Entree prices start at: $12.00
All major credit cards accepted

Now in its 20th year, **LUCIA'S** provides
serious Italian cuisine emphasizing food from
the region of Abruzzi, Italy. Its unique
atmosphere includes intimate booths, roses
on the tables and a wonderful fresco ceiling.
The service is efficient and cordial. Available
for private parties and events.

Open Daily
Lunch: 11:30AM-3PM (Fri., Sat., Sun.)
Dinner: 4PM-11PM

MAMMA MARIA

3 North Street
(617) 523-0077

Reservations: Recommended
Valet parking available
Casual attire
Entree prices start at: $18.00
All major credit cards accepted

Now in its tenth year, **MAMMA MARIA** has
evolved into one of Boston's premier fine dining
establishments. It's a unique three-story
townhouse which offers elegant dining for its
discerning clientele and provides an intimate
atmosphere within its six small dining rooms.
Many rooms have views and there is a lovely
glass-enclosed terrace on the second floor
overlooking North Square. Available for
private parties and events.

Hours: 5PM-9:30PM (Sun.-Thurs.)
5PM-10:30PM (Fri.-Sat.)

MANGIA-MANGIA

147 Endicott Street
(617) 523-1768

Reservations not accepted
Casual attire
Prices start at $2.25
Credit cards not accepted

MANGIA-MANGIA is an Italian fast food establishment. They offer a wonderful variety of subs, including steak and cheese, chicken cutlet parmesan, and meatball. They boast Boston's best cheeseburger, aptly named the "Mangia-burger." Breakfast is robust and filling.

Breakfast: 6AM-11:30AM
Lunch: 6AM-3:30PM
Closed Sunday

MARCUCCIO'S

125 Salem Street
(617) 723-1807

Reservations: Recommended
Casual attire
Entree prices start at: $17.00
VISA/MC

MARCUCCIO'S has a funky, lower Manhattan, Soho atmosphere which offers fresh, simply prepared Italian fare that is true to the soul of Italian cooking. Careful attention is paid to flavor and presentation. The environment is urbane, yet relaxed. You will find enjoyable dining at a price that is an additional delight. Available for private parties and events.

Hours: 5PM-10PM (Sun.-Thurs.)
5PM-11PM (Fri.-Sat.)

MASIMINO'S CUCINA ITALIANA

207 Endicott Street
(617) 523-5959

Reservations not accepted
Casual attire
Entree prices start at: $8.00
All major credit cards accepted

MASIMINO'S has won numerous national and international awards for their cuisine. Their lasagna is delicious and hardy. Daily specials are offered. Be prepared for very good food at very good prices. Usually closed Sunday, they are open if there is a Celtics or Bruins game.

Hours: 11AM-10PM (Mon.-Thurs.)
11AM-11PM (Fri.-Sat.)

MAURIZIO'S

364 Hanover Street
(617) 367-1123

Reservations: Recommended Sun.-Fri.
Casual attire
Entree prices start at: $16.00
All major credit cards accepted

Chef-owned, and winner of the "Best Seafood Stew" at the International Fish Bowl, 1996, **MAURIZIO'S** features excellent Southern Italian food. The Mediterranean cuisine includes whole fish on the grill, rack of lamb, steak, filet mignon, veal, chicken and pork. The atmosphere is very comfortable and inviting.

Lunch: 12noon-3PM (Wed.-Sat.)
Dinner: 5PM-10PM (Sun.-Sat.)
Closed Monday

MONICA'S KITCHEN

67 Prince Street

Casual attire
VISA/MC

This family-owned restaurant caters to those
who desire Italian comfort food for dining
in or take-out. Specialties include homemade
pasta, roasted meats, seafood, chicken,
roasted potatoes and homemade salads.
Select from **MONICA'S** delicious variety
of Italian-style cuisine and pay by the pound!
A great concept!

Open daily
11AM-9PM

MONICA'S RESTAURANT

143-145 Richmond St.
(617) 720-5472

Reservations not accepted
Casual attire
Entree prices start at: $9.95
VISA/MC

MONICA'S is known for being the
quintessential family-owned Italian restaurant,
offering traditional fare with a unique twist.
All pasta is made on the premises. Generous
portions are served in this relaxed and
pleasant restaurant. Beer and wine available.

Open Daily
5PM-10PM

MOTHER ANNA'S

211 Hanover Street
(617) 523-8496

Reservations: Recommended
Casual attire
Entree prices start at: $7.95
All major credit cards accepted

Four generations have consistently offered delicious, imaginative Italian food in sizable portions. Its convenient location on the corner of Hanover St. and Cross St. makes this restaurant a very popular place! **MOTHER ANNA'S** staff is gracious and efficient.

Open Daily
Lunch: 11:30AM-3:30PM
Dinner: 3:30PM-11:30PM

NICOLE RISTORANTE

54 Salem Street
(617) 742-6999

Reservations: Recommended
Casual attire
Entree prices start at: $9.95
All major credit cards accepted

A warm and romantic atmosphere surrounds
you at **NICOLE**. White linen tablecloths with
pink napkins add to the ambiance. The
innovative menu highlights every region of
Italy. There are delicious selections to appeal
to every taste, including pasta, chicken, veal,
fish, steaks and chops. Daily specials.
Available for private parties and events.

Lunch: 11:30AM-2:30PM (Thurs.-Sat.)
Dinner: 4PM-10PM (Tues.-Sat.)
3PM-9PM (Sun.)
Closed Monday

NORTH STREET GRILLE AND CAFE

229 North Street
(617) 523-9495

Reservations not accepted
Casual attire
Entree prices start at: $8.95
AMEX, VISA/MC

This family-style restaurant boasts serving the "Best Breakfast in Boston." The innovative menu offers many specialties, some of which include: Buffalo wings, chicken quesadillas, killer nachos, a great Reuben, exceptional burgers, chicken marsala, broiled scrod, and fish and chips. Beer and wine available. From the Paul Revere house, go toward the top of North Square. Turn right onto Sun Court. **NORTH STREET GRILLE** is directly across the street.

Open Daily
8AM-10PM (Mon.-Fri.)
7AM-10PM (Sat.-Sun.)

PAT'S PUSHCART RESTAURANT

61 Endicott Street
(617) 523-9616

Reservations: Recommended
Casual attire
Entree prices start at: $7.50
VISA/MC

PAT'S PUSHCART is a family owned and operated restaurant which has been serving the public for 26 years. Many specialties are offered in a very warm and friendly setting. Try the chicken angelique (folded breast of chicken stuffed with prosciutto and mozzarella in tomato sauce), or chicken villanese (chicken strips with clams and mushrooms with red or white sauce over pasta.) Available for private parties and events.

Hours: 5PM-10:30PM (Tues.-Sat.)
Closed Sun. and Mon.

PICCOLA VENEZIA

263 Hanover Street
(617) 523-3888

Reservations: Recommended
Casual attire
Entree prices start at: $7.95
All major credit cards accepted

PICCOLA VENEZIA is a gutsy, old-fashioned Italian restaurant serving home-style food in a casual environment. Special dishes include arancini, fried baccala, baked ziti, and pork chops with a balsamic glaze. There is a challenging Godfather platter heaped with veal, chicken cutlets, eggplant, meatballs and sausages. For dessert, try a brandy-laced tiramisu, which is said to be the best in the North End. Available for private parties and events.

Open daily
Lunch: 11AM-4PM
Dinner: 4PM-10PM

PICCOLO NIDO

257 North Street
(617) 742-4272

Reservations: Recommended
Casual attire
Entree prices start at: $14.95
All major credit cards accepted

PICCOLO NIDO'S selections have a nice balance of regional Italian dishes. Their menu changes twice a year for an interesting variety of cuisine. Using only the freshest products available, their motto is "fresh and simple." It is a warm, comfortable and romantic dining experience with attentive servers. Available for private parties and events.

Hours: 4PM-11PM (Mon.-Sat.)
Closed Sunday

PIZZA RELLA

417 Hanover Street
(617) 742-7172

Reservations not accepted
Casual attire
Entree prices start at: $4.15
All major credit cards accepted

PIZZA RELLA welcomes families to their restaurant. They serve a selection of pizza, pasta, sandwiches and calzones. Additionally, a grilled chicken or grilled sausage dinner, each with a salad, is available for $7.95. The food is good and the service is efficient and friendly.

Hours: 4PM-10PM (Mon.-Thurs.)
11AM-11PM (Fri.,Sat.,Sun.)

PIZZERIA REGINA

11 1/2 Thatcher Street
(617) 227-0765

Casual attire
Prices start at: $5.49 small pizza
$9.29 large pizza
Credit cards not accepted

Since 1926, **PIZZERIA REGINA** has been greeting customers with a hearty welcome to "Boston's Original Pizzeria." It's a tradition that REGINA'S brick oven pizza is made with only fresh, natural ingredients, special seasonings, and a unique blend of cheeses shredded by hand. The Polcari family is proud to serve their delicious pizza with your choice of beer, wine or soda. A fun place!

Hours: 11AM-11:30PM (Mon.-Thurs.)
11AM-Midnight (Fri.-Sat.)
Noon-11PM (Sun.)

POMODORO

319 Hanover Street
(617) 367-4348

Reservations: Recommended
Casual attire
Entree prices start at: $13.95
Credit cards not accepted

POMODORO is a lively, popular restaurant
specializing is contemporary Northern Italian
food. A few of the entrees on the menu include
Seafood fra diavalo with pasta, mussels
marinara with pasta, fried calamari with gravy,
and chicken carbonara with wild
mushrooms, Italian ham and cracked black
pepper tossed over rigatoni. Available
for private parties and events.

Open daily
11am-11pm

PUSHCART CAFFÉ

115 Salem Street
(617) 523-8123

Casual attire
Entree prices start at: $5.00
Credit cards not accepted

When the weather permits, the windows open wide in this cheery cafe. Cigars are sold, making it a "cigar friendly" place. **PUSHCART CAFFÉ** serves hot and cold subs, salads, pasta, pizza and desserts. Beverage selections include cappuccino, espresso, mocha latte, beer, wine and cordials plus delicious ice cream frappes. Families are welcome.

Open Daily
11AM-Midnight
Closed Monday

RABIA'S RESTAURANT

73 Salem Street
(617) 227-6637

Reservations: Recommended
Casual attire
Entree prices start at: $12.00
All major credit cards accepted

As you walk into **RABIA'S,** you will experience
a country Italian environment. Fresh flowers and
candles on linen tablecloths express the quality
of the dining. If the weather permits, the
windows open for a pleasant breeze. The
innovative cuisine is both Northern and
Southern Italian and each plate is a work of art.
Home-made ravioli is a specialty.
There is an extensive wine list.

Open Daily
Lunch: 11AM-3PM
Dinner: 4PM-11PM

RICARDO'S RISTORANTE

175 North Street
(617) 720-3994

Reservations: Recommended
Casual attire
Entree prices start at: $7.95
AMEX, VISA/MC, DINERS

RICARDO'S is a traditional Italian Ristorante
which offers home-made fare in an airy, cordial,
contemporary setting. One of the excellent
specialties is stuffed calamari over linguine.
Enjoy this or another enticing dish from the
extensive and affordable menu. Top notch
service. Specials are offered every day.
Available for private parties and events.

Open Daily
Lunch: 11:30AM-3PM
Dinner: 3PM-10PM

RISTORANTE BELLA VISTA

288 Hanover Street
(617) 367-4999

Reservations: Recommended
Casual attire
Entree prices start at: $7.95
AMEX

You will enjoy the solid cuisine and excellent service at **BELLA VISTA.** This traditional restaurant is charming and comfortable and offers an exciting menu with lobster fra diavolo and shrimp and scallops diavolo as specialties of the house.

Open Daily
Lunch: 11:30AM-2PM
Dinner: 2PM-11:30PM

RISTORANTE EUNO

119 Salem Street
(617) 573-9406

Reservations: Recommended
Casual attire
Entree prices start at: $14.00
AMEX, VISA/MC

Before you step through the hand-carved front door, notice the 200 year old terra-cotta roof tiles decorating the facade of **RISTORANTE EUNO**. With exposed brick ceilings and walls, a warm rustic feeling exists throughout the restaurant. Downstairs, you'll find a bar and a quaint stone fireplace. Sicilian-Mediterranean peasant cuisine is offered along with a selection of organic meats and vegetables. The olive oil comes from the family grove in Filetto, Italy. Available for private parties and events.

Lunch: 11:30AM-3PM (Sat.-Sun.)
Dinner: 5PM-10PM (Sun.-Thurs.)
5PM-11PM (Fri.-Sat.)

RISTORANTE ROSINA

379 Hanover Street
(617) 523-8481

Reservations: Recommended
Valet parking available
Casual attire
Entree prices start at: $10.00
All major credit cards accepted

The look and feel of **RISTORANTE ROSINA**
is charming. In summer and good weather,
the sliding glass windows open to make the
restaurant feel as if you are dining outside.
The kitchen turns out specialties from all
regions of Italy. They serve a delicious chicken
rosina. It is best described as casual, fine
dining in a relaxed atmosphere. Available
for private parties and events.

Hours: 5PM-10PM (Mon.-Thurs.)
5PM-11PM (Fri.-Sat.)
Noon-10PM (Sun.)

RISTORANTE SARACENO

286 Hanover Street
(617) 227-5888

Reservations: Recommended
Casual attire
Entree prices start at: $9.95
AMEX, VISA/MC, DINERS

SARACENO is charming, upscale, and
exemplifies old world charm. A wonderful
Neapolitan menu is offered consisting of veal
chops, shrimp, tuna, swordfish, lasagna, pasta
and more. It is complete with a charming
rooftop garden room. Available for private
parties and events.

Open Daily
Lunch: Noon-3PM
Dinner: 3PM-10:30PM

SABATINO'S

95 North Washington Street
(617) 742-3665

Reservations: Recommended
Casual attire
Entree prices start at: $7.95
AMEX, VISA/MC

Bringing you the flavor of Italy with the hospitality of the North End, **SABATINO'S** aims to please their customers. The diverse menu is wonderful, but if you crave an item not on the menu, the chef will try to accomodate you. One of the house specialties is veal saltimbocca. Casual and friendly, you'll enjoy this 32 seat restaurant. Daily specials. Available for private parties and events.

Hours: 11:30AM-10PM (Tues.-Wed., Thurs.)
11:30AM-10:30PM (Fri.-Sat.)
11:30AM-9PM (Sun.)
Closed Monday

SAGE

69 Price Street
(617) 248-8814

Reservations: Recommended
Casual attire
Entree prices start at: $16.00
AMEX, VISA/MC, DISCOVER

Hospitality reigns at **SAGE**. It is a cozy, trattoria-like restaurant. Locals and critics rave about the food which is presented to appeal to your eye as well as your appetite. The exceptional innovative cuisine and warm atmosphere bring a touch of Italy to your evening.

Open Daily
5PM-10PM (Sun.-Thurs.)
5PM-10:30PM (Fri.-Sat.)

STANZA dei SIGARI

296 Hanover Street
(617) 227-0295

Reservations not accepted
Casual attire
All major credit cards accepted

Located at the **CAFFÉ VITTORIA, STANZA dei SIGARI** is a cigar museum featuring quality cigars, gourmet appetizers and the finest liqueurs from around the world. Smokers can enjoy a good stogie with impunity. For those who don't want to experience smoke, there are non-smoking areas. Cigars are priced from $8.-$50., drinks from $7.-$160.

Open Daily
5PM-1AM

TERRAMIA RISTORANTE

98 Salem Street
(617) 523-3112

Reservations: Recommended
Casual attire
Entree prices start at: $9.50
All major credit cards accepted

Chef Mario Nocera won Boston's 1996 Edible
Art Award for the most creative and delicious
dish. The 40 seat **TERRAMIA** attracts repeat
customers who enjoy this comfortable
restaurant which offers plentiful food at
modest prices and friendly, personal service.

Hours: 5PM-10PM (Mon.-Thurs.)
5PM-10:30PM (Fri.)
4PM-10:30PM (Sat.)
1PM-10PM (Sun.)

THE DAILY CATCH

323 Hanover Street
(617) 523-8567

Reservations: Not accepted
Casual attire
Entree prices start at: $10.25
Credit cards not accepted

THE DAILY CATCH is a one room eatery with kitchen and dining together. Opened in 1973, it's a casual, family owned restaurant specializing in serving local fish (fish and shellfish), with Sicilian style recipes. House specialties are calamari served either fried, marinated, sautéed or grilled, lobster fra diavolo for two, and black squid ink pasta.

Open Daily
11:30AM-11:30PM (Fri.-Sat.)
11:30AM-10PM (Sun.-Thurs.)

THEO'S COZY CORNER RESTAURANT

162 Salem Street
(617) 241-0202

Reservations: Not accepted
Casual attire
Entree prices start at: $5.00
Credit cards not accepted

This a prime example of a genuine corner Italian restaurant. Whether a tourist or a local, you will be welcomed by the very friendly staff. On weekends, breakfast is served all day. There is a $4.25 "super special" which includes a bottomless cup of coffee. Italian dinners cooked to order. **THEO'S** has take-out and local delivery. Families are welcome.

6:30AM-3PM (Mon.)
6:30AM-8:30PM (Tues.-Fri.)
6:30AM-3PM (Sat.)
6:30AM-2PM (Sun.)

TRATTORIA Á SCALINATELLA

253 Hanover Street
(617) 742-8240

Reservations: Necessary
Upscale, casual attire
Entree prices start at: $13.95
AMEX, VISA/MC

TRATTORIA Á SCALINATELLA is located on the second floor away from street level noise. It's a small, rustic and very romantic dining establishment. A working fireplace warms every winter evening, and it's a favorite destination for celebrities. The staff is from Italy and is very knowledgeable about food selections from all regions of Italy. They offer the most extensive wine portfolio in Boston. The signature dish is the veal chop. All pasta is handmade.

Open Daily
5PM-11PM

TRATTORIA IL PANINO

11 Parmenter Street
(617) 720-1336

Reservations not accepted
Casual attire
Entree prices start at: $9.95
Credit cards not accepted

The ORIGINAL **IL PANINO** serves a variety of specialties fresh from the open kitchen directly to your table. Seafood, veal, pasta, ravioli and vegetable antipasto are a sampling of the tasty menu. Enjoy a delightful Italian wine from the extensive wine list in a comfortable, casual trattoria setting. Part of the Trattoria Il Panino restaurant group.

Open Daily
Lunch: 11:30AM-3:30PM
Dinner: 4PM-11PM

TRATTORIA LORENZO

48-50 Salem Street
(617) 227-6444

Reservations not accepted
Casual attire
Entree prices start at: $8.00
AMEX, VISA/MC, TRANSMEDIA

Conveniently located on the corner of Salem Street and Cross Street, **TRATTORIA LORENZO** is a popular place! Friendly and upbeat, with an Italian flavor, several of the cozy booths upstairs have a fabulous view of downtown Boston. Featured dishes are osso bucco (braised veal shafts); roasted cod with roasted tomatoes, black olives and capers; mushroom filled ravioli; and gourmet pizza. All pasta is homemade. House specials offered daily. Available for private parties and events.

Lunch:11:30AM-4PM (Mon.-Sat.)
Dinner: 4PM-10PM (Mon.-Thurs.)
4PM-11PM (Fri.-Sat.)
Closed Sunday

TUTTO MARE

63 Salem Street
(617) 557-6064

Reservations: Recommended for 6 or more
Casual attire
Entree prices start at: $10.95
AMEX, VISA/MC

A uniquely exciting restaurant, **TUTTO MARE** specializes in seafood. Covering the top of a colorful aquarium, there is a fabulous presentation of fresh seafood on ice. Appetizers include scallops, cherrystones, octopus salad or caviar. The extensive menu features swordfish, yellowtail snapper, monkfish, or lobster. The service is meticulous at this 48 seat restaurant. Part of the Trattoria Il Panino restaurant group.

Hours: 4PM-11PM (Mon.-Fri.)
4PM-11:30PM (Sat.)
3PM-10PM (Sun.)

VADOPAZZO (ENOTECA)
241 Hanover Street
(617) 248-6800

Reservations: Recommended
Casual attire
Entree prices start at: $9.95
AMEX, VISA/MC, TRANSMEDIA

VADOPAZZO'S chefs are from Naples, Italy.
Featured are 12 types of risotto, a tasty wood-
fired brick oven pizza, on-premise made pasta,
and steak. Specializing in fine Italian wines,
there is an in-house sommelier, an enoteca
(wine library), with a computerized wine information system and a wine reserve cellar. If you
are a cigar smoker, the cigar room awaits you!
Part of the Trattoria Il Panino restaurant group.
Available for private parties and events.

Hours: 5PM-11PM (Mon.-Fri.)
2PM-Midnight (Sat.)
2PM-11PM (Sun.)

VILLA-FRANCESCA

150 Richmond Street
(617) 367-2948

Reservations: Recommended
Valet parking available
Casual attire
Entree prices start at: $14.95
AMEX, VISA/MC, DINERS

VILLA-FRANCESCA is a charming
restaurant in the heart of the North End.
A singer entertains Wednesday, Thursday, and
Saturday evening. A delicious house specialty
is veal valdestana (8 ounces of veal stuffed with
prosciutto and fontina cheese seasoned with
bread crumbs and prepared in red wine sauce
with mushrooms). Available for private
parties and events.

Open Daily
Lunch: 11:30AM-3PM
Dinner: 5PM-12:30AM